Ancient
Pueblo

Archaeology Unlocks the
Secrets of America's Past

Ancient
Pueblo

Archaeology Unlocks the
Secrets of America's Past

By Anita Croy

J. Jefferson Reid, Consultant

NATIONAL
GEOGRAPHIC
Washington, DC

Contents

< This ancient Pueblo petroglyph, or drawing scratched into rock, shows two warriors.
At lower left, one holds a shield decorated with bear paws.

< Cliff Palace, at Mesa Verde in Arizona, was built by the Anasazi in about 1200. Today it is the most visited archaeological site in the United States.

The past is like a foreign country, and there are only three ways to go there. One path is through documents—letters, journals, old photographs, and books. These accounts preserve events and emotions about past lives.

Another way to reach the past is through personal memory or oral history passed down from grandparents to parents to children. This is the path most often taken by the modern descendants of the Ancestral Pueblo. Their past lives today in language, daily life, and their relation to the land, still vibrant after so many centuries.

A third path is the study of artifacts and the ruins left by people on the landscape. This is the path taken by archaeologists, and in this book you will learn how they explored the lives of the Ancestral Pueblo. The past does not stand still, and the secrets of yesterday become the accepted facts of today. Each time archaeologists travel this path, old questions are answered by new scientific techniques, and the Pueblo past seems clearer than before. And like going to a foreign country, different archaeologists have different views of what the Pueblo past was like. Through ruins and documents, this book will take you down archaeology's path, but your view of the Pueblo past will be your own, and you will create your own memories of ancient life and peoples through what you will learn.

J. Jefferson Reid
Arizona, 2007

▽ J. Jefferson Reid examines Canyon Creek Cliff Dwelling in Arizona. The site was occupied in the early 1300s, possibly by a combination of Anasazi and Mogollon.

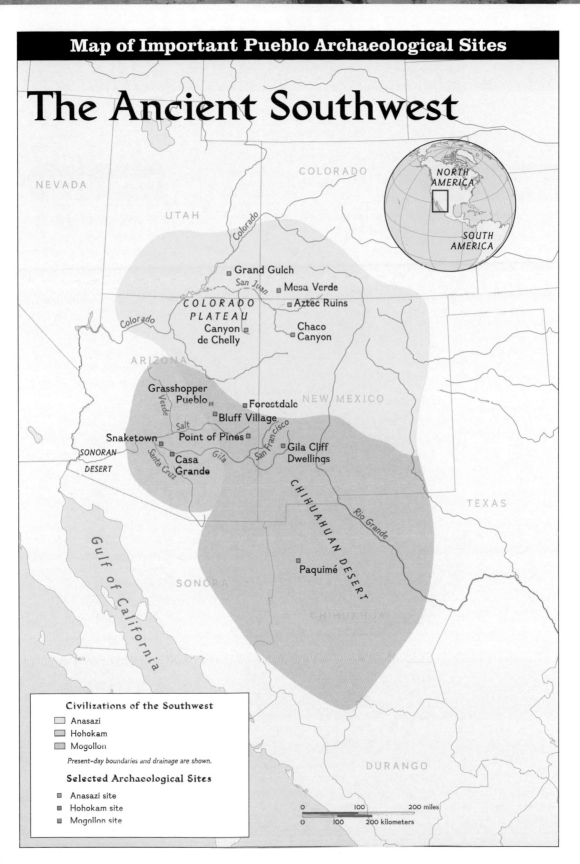

Map of Important Pueblo Archaeological Sites

The Ancient Southwest

NORTH AMERICA

SOUTH AMERICA

NEVADA

COLORADO

UTAH

Colorado

Grand Gulch

San Juan

Mesa Verde

COLORADO PLATEAU

Aztec Ruins

Colorado

Canyon de Chelly

Chaco Canyon

ARIZONA

NEW MEXICO

Grasshopper Pueblo

Verde

Forestdale

Bluff Village

Salt

Snaketown

Point of Pines

San Francisco

SONORAN DESERT

Santa Cruz

Gila

Casa Grande

Gila Cliff Dwellings

TEXAS

Rio Grande

Gulf of California

CHIHUAHUAN DESERT

SONORA

Paquimé

CHIHUAHUA

DURANGO

Civilizations of the Southwest

- Anasazi
- Hohokam
- Mogollon

Present-day boundaries and drainage are shown.

Selected Archaeological Sites

- Anasazi site
- Hohokam site
- Mogollon site

0   100   200 miles

0   100   200 kilometers

THREE GROUPS OF
Ancestral Pueblo

Hohokam

ca A.D. 200—1450

The Hohokam were farmers who lived in the desert areas along the Gila and Salt rivers in what is now southern Arizona. They dug an extensive network of canals to carry water to fields where they grew crops to support their people. The Hohokam had trading links across a wide area, and were skilled potters. Some experts argue that the Hohokam were the ancestors of a number of modern groups of Native Americans, including the Tohono O'Odham and the Pima of Arizona.

Anasazi

ca A.D. 100—1600

The Anasazi were a group of Ancestral Pueblo who lived on the Colorado Plateau around the area now known as Four Corners. Originally skilled basketmakers who lived a largely nomadic lifestyle, they later settled in large, multi-roomed buildings called pueblos, which may have been social and ritual centers. They were astronomers who studied the movement of the sun to follow the changing seasons. Later Anasazi settlements were often built high on cliff faces that could only be reached by a dangerous climb.

< A Hohokam bowl with the design of a turtle

Timeline of Pueblo History

A.D. 250	500	750	1000

ca 200
Emergence of semi-nomadic communities in the Southwest

ca 300
The Hohokam begin building canals

ca 600 The Anasazi begin to create pottery vessels rather than baskets

ca 900
Building begins at Chaco Canyon

ca 1030
Chaco Canyon enters its golden age

< These Anasazi spear points were used to hunt game for meat to supplement the crops grown by farmers.

Mogollon

ca A.D. 200—1400

The Mogollon is the name given to the Pueblo who lived on highlands in the area that is now Arizona, New Mexico, and Mexico. They originally lived in pit houses partly buried in the ground, but later built larger pueblos which they supported through farming. The Mimbres branch of the Mogollon produced beautiful pottery. The Mogollon became less distinctive, and may have merged with the Anasazi. Some experts doubt that the Mogollon were a separate culture at all, but think they were always linked with the Anasazi and the Hohokam.

> An Anasazi vase based on the distinctive black and white pattern of Mimbres pottery

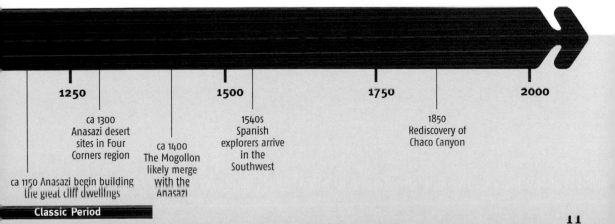

1250

ca 1300
Anasazi desert
sites in Four
Corners region

ca 1400
The Mogollon
likely merge
with the
Anasazi

ca 1150 Anasazi begin building
the great cliff dwellings

Classic Period

1500

1540s
Spanish
explorers arrive
in the
Southwest

1750

1850
Rediscovery of
Chaco Canyon

2000

Yesterday Comes Alive

CHAPTER 1

How do we learn what we know about the past?

Stephen Lekson loves to hike through the deserts of the American Southwest. The professor from the University of Colorado at Boulder has spent the last twenty years exploring the region and studying its ancient ruins. Few people live in the desert today, but at one time it was home to large communities. These people belonged to the Pueblo, the name now given to a number of different groups of Native Americans who once lived in the Southwest and whose descendants still live there. The ancient Pueblo, who are sometimes known as the Ancestral Pueblo, had a reputation as peaceful

< Tucked beneath the massive face of Canyon de Chelly in Arizona, the dwelling called the White House looks small—yet its eighty rooms were once home to an entire Pueblo community.

farmers who lived in societies without rulers. They built stone houses in canyons and beneath cliffs. After they had dominated the whole of the Colorado Plateau in the A.D. 1100s, however, the Pueblo suddenly left. Across an area of about 30,000 square miles (78,000 sq km), they abandoned their communities almost overnight.

Why the Pueblo left is one of the biggest mysteries in archaeology. Lekson thinks he may know the answer. He argues that the Pueblo did have rulers—and that power struggles among rulers led the whole people to move south to a new site, Paquimé, in present-day Chihuahua, Mexico.

< Decorated pottery is one of the most useful clues for studying the Pueblo.

Disputed theory

Lekson's theory is highly controversial. Many scholars disagree that Paquimé was built by the same people as the centers farther north. Other scholars disagree with Lekson's view that life had become more violent as Pueblo society began to break up. The modern Pueblo, who claim descent from the ancient peoples of the Southwest, also reject the suggestion that their ancestors' lifestyles were violent.

∨ Archaeologists scramble up to a cliff-top ruin in Utah. The toeholds that once led up the rock face have been worn away.

Lekson is just one of the scholars trying to solve the mysteries about the peoples who once lived in present-day Arizona, Colorado, New Mexico, and Utah. Although experts have learned much about them since the remains of their sites were first studied in the 19th century, there is a lot more that they do not know. The best hope of finding out is through the work of archaeologists, history's detectives. Archaeologists study remains of the past in great detail so that they can piece together even tiny clues into a picture of how people once lived.

Who were the Pueblo?

But which people? The people of the Southwest did not call themselves the Pueblo. Pueblo is a Spanish word that means "village." The first Spanish explorers arrived in the Southwest in the 16th century. In Arizona they found remarkable sites: multi-story buildings and stone ruins of settlements that looked like villages. The Spaniards assumed that the ruins were the work of the ancestors of Native Americans still living in the area. They named the people "Pueblo"—and the name stuck.

It was not accurate, however. Modern Pueblo include different groups, such as the Rio Grande

Pueblo, the Hopi, and the Zuni. The ancient Pueblo who began to farm in the region in about 1500 B.C. also included different groups. From studying ruins and artifacts, archaeologists have identified three main cultural groups: the Hohokam, the Anasazi, and the Mogollon. Each group was made up of smaller groups, which archaeologists often name for the places where they lived.

∧ Experts think that symbols such as the handprints in this Pueblo rock painting probably had special meaning—but no one knows what.

Canal builders

One of the three groups was the Hohokam. In the language of their modern descendants, the Tohono O'Odham, Hohokam means "that which perished." They lived in the Sonoran Desert of what is now southern Arizona. In valleys along

∧ Water was the key to living in the generally dry Southwest. Grand Gulch in Utah supported many Pueblo communities along its 60 miles (100 km).

> An archaeologist makes notes next to the wall of an Anasazi pueblo.

the Gila and Salt Rivers, they built irrigation systems to allow them to farm. Emil Haury, a pioneer of archaeology in the Southwest, suggested that the Hohokam had arrived from Mexico, but modern archaeologists mainly reject the theory. The Hohokam disappeared near the end of the 15th century.

Mountain dwellers

The Mogollon lived in forested mountains of the Chihuahuan Desert basins of southeastern Arizona, southern New Mexico, and western

Texas, as well as northern Mexico. They farmed, but also hunted and gathered food from the forests.

For a long time, experts did not recognize the Mogollon as a separate culture—some still do not. The houses and artifacts they created before A.D. 700 were hard to tell apart from those of the Hohokam. Later, however, the Mogollon built pit houses sunk into the ground, and made beautiful black and white pottery called Mimbres pottery for the group who created it. After about 1300, Mogollon culture again became less distinctive. The people had likely come under the influence of the most famous Pueblo culture, the Anasazi.

The ancient Anasazi

The Anasazi occupied the desert region around what is now known as Four Corners, where the states of Arizona, Colorado, New Mexico, and Utah meet. The most populated regions—Chaco Canyon in New Mexico and Mesa Verde in Colorado—are today two of the most visited archaeological sites in the United States. Mesa Verde alone is home to at least 600 Anasazi sites, with more still being discovered.

The physical evidence shows that the Anasazi emerged in about A.D. 100 and left Four Corners about 1500 years later. Over time they moved from site to site, building new settlements

∧ This apron was woven by an Anasazi basketmaker from flexible branches and plant fibers.

in canyons and beneath sheltered cliff sides. They dominated the Colorado Plateau between 900 and 1150.

The 12-mile-long (19-km) Chaco Canyon in northwest New Mexico is home to the Anasazi's largest constructions. The so-called "great houses"—Pueblo Bonito, Chetro Ketl, and Pueblo Alto—all lie in the canyon or on the nearby mesas. These many-roomed buildings were so large that they may have been used for shared

Trees that tell stories

One useful technique for dating the Pueblo is dendrochronology. It relies on the fact that a slice through a tree trunk reveals a series of rings, one for each year the tree has lived. Astronomer Andrew E. Douglass realized that the rings reveal not only the age of the tree but also how much rainfall it got in particular years. A wider ring meant lots of rain, while a narrow ring meant drought. The breakthrough revealed a lot about the Anasazi and Mogollon, and the conditions in which they lived. It was more difficult to learn about the Hohokam: The wood in their homes came from trees that were more difficult to date using dendrochronology.

∧ Dr. Tom Swetnam of the University of Arizona studies rings in cross sections of different trees.

communal ceremonies. Experts such as Stephen Lekson, however, argue that they may have been palaces for the society's leaders. No one knows their purpose for sure.

Mesa Verde may have been chosen as a site for settlement because it was hidden away. That suggests that the people may have faced some kind of threat. Although most archaeologists do not believe that warfare played a part in the Anasazi's disappearance after 1300, Lekson and others are challenging that view.

Reading the clues

In this book you will discover how experts have learned about the Ancestral Pueblo. In Chapter 2, you will see how even small clues like tiny flakes of rock can change our view of a culture. You will also see how the

Hohokam carved and painted artwork onto rocks throughout their lands. Some artwork is realistic. Others are patterns that may have had a spiritual meaning.

Chapter 3 reveals the importance of physical remains to the study of the Pueblo. At the largest Anasazi cliff dwelling, the Cliff Palace at Mesa Verde, stand tall buildings and round rooms dug into the ground. When it was first discovered about 120 years ago, the site still contained the remains of corncobs, tassels, and shucks, and even a few kernels of corn that had been overlooked by rats. The ruin was in a very poor state. Some walls had fallen down and stones blocked passages.

Please don't touch!

Many clues to life in the Southwest have vanished. Early discoverers of ancient ruins did not appreciate how valuable even tiny pieces of material might be in revealing the past. They took objects to sell them, rather than passing them to experts to be examined. The science of archaeology was just beginning—there were few experts who could analyze the finds.

Today, archaeologists understand the importance of examining where objects are found.

Often they can learn a lot from which objects are found together. Objects tend to be grouped together in strata, or layers that build up in the earth. The oldest layers, at the bottom, are buried as more soil and debris settles on top of them. The layer in which objects are found reveals when they were made.

A changing picture

In Chapter 4 you will see how much is still left to learn about the Pueblo. It was only in the middle of the 20th century that experts pieced together enough clues to learn that the Mogollon were once a separate culture— and some people still dispute that fact. You will also learn more about Stephen Lekson, who explains the thinking behind some of his ideas. Those theories challenge what we think we know about the Ancestral Pueblo. Who knows how many more discoveries are still waiting to be made?

< Descendants of the Pueblo still live in communal homes and grow similar crops to their vanished ancestors.

Farmers in the Desert

CHAPTER 2

How did the Hohokam support their people?

Steven Shackley is a puzzle solver. It seems odd to him that the Hohokam only lived in one small area as many archaeologists believe. The expert from the University of California at Berkeley thinks that that was unlikely. The clue to the puzzle, he thinks, lies in flakes of glassy black stone scattered over the red soil of the Sonoran Desert. This is obsidian, which was widely used in the ancient world to make blades and other sharp tools.

< This design from a Hohokam pot seems to show people dancing; the dancers with what looks like long hair may be wearing ritual headdresses.

HOHOKAM
ca A.D. 200 – 1450

0   A.D. 1000   A.D. 2000

21

A remarkable kind of rock

Obsidian, the black, glasslike stone that Steven Shackley is using to study the Hohokam, is very useful for archaeologists. It was widely used in the ancient world to make tools and blades, because it is very hard and can be made very sharp. Obsidian comes only from volcanoes, and experts can trace obsidian to particular volcanoes.

< Obsidian is so shiny it was sometimes used to make jewelry.

Because the stone was traded widely, it is very useful for tracing how trade networks spread.

Obsidian is also useful because it contains its own dating mechanism. When a flake is chipped off a piece of obsidian, the new surface begins to interact with chemicals in the air. The interaction forms a thin layer on the stone, called a rind, which gets thicker over time. By measuring the thickness of the rind, it is possible to work out when a piece of obsidian was first shaped. However, dating a sample in this way is very difficult and may be inaccurate. Experts also need to get dates in other ways for comparison.

Shackley's evidence showed that the Hohokam had used obsidian—but it showed something else, too. Flakes of the stone are scattered throughout present-day Arizona. Shackley has analyzed obsidian throughout the area

and learned that it came from a number of different sources. That suggests to him that the Hohokam had

V The Salt River, here flowing through its canyon in Arizona, lay at the heart of the Hohokam irrigation system.

∧ A Hohokam artist scratched this near-perfect spiral into a rock in the Arizona desert—but modern experts can only guess at the meaning of the symbol.

a well-developed system for trading goods such as obsidian among different areas of settlement and even among different peoples.

Shackley has traced obsidian points—used on hunting spears—west as far as modern-day California and south to what is now the border with Mexico. He suggests that the ancient Patayan people who lived in the Imperial Valley in California may have been related to the Hohokam.

Changing views

Shackley's theory changed the accepted view of the Hohokam. Their trading network covered a region of at least 50,000 square miles (129,500 sq km). He argues that this large area included people from different ethnic backgrounds who spoke different languages, but who all shared the same culture. That suggestion in turn throws new light on the origins of some modern Native Americans. The Hohokam were already known to be the ancestors of the Tohono O'Odham and the Pima of Arizona. Now it turns out that they might be the ancestors of other native groups, too.

Shackley believes that the Hohokam have been overshadowed by

> Stone palettes like this sometimes turn up in Hohokam burial grounds. They may have been used to grind powder to make face paints.

other ancient Pueblo. He believes that people are often so impressed by the spectacular cliff palaces of the Anasazi, for example, that they do not give the Hohokam the credit they deserve. In Shackley's view, the Hohokam were the most advanced of all the Southwestern civilizations.

How did the Hohokam live?

The Hohokam faced some of the most challenging environments of any of the Pueblo. They settled in the Sonoran Desert and the dry valleys of south–central Arizona, near where the city of Phoenix now stands. Today the soil is dry and hard, and only cactuses and other desert plants grow, but more rivers once threaded the deserts.

Many of the rivers have now dried up, but they allowed the Hohokam to overcome the problem of rainfall that in some places was less than four inches (ten cm) a year. The Hohokam built the most sophisticated system of canals north of Mexico City.

The achievement of the Hohokam was remarkable. They had no metal tools, no wheels, and no animals they could use to move large amounts of soil. Yet the Hohokam were able to

< An image of a bird painted onto a piece of Hohokam pottery: Such artwork may have had a ritual meaning, helping to bring good hunting, for example.

∧ Visitors examine the walls of a Hohokam canal excavated in Arizona. The Hohokam built their canals with tools made from stone and wood.

build hundreds of miles of canals over nearly a thousand years beginning in about A.D. 300.

Canals in the desert

The Hohokam built their canals along three rivers, the Salt, Gila, and Verde. The most advanced system was built along the Salt River in a valley near the location of modern-day Phoenix. Some canals carried water up to 16 miles (25 km) into the desert. This allowed the Hohokam to move farther away from the rivers. As well as watering fields to grow crops, the water was also used for drinking, cooking, and pottery making.

The total network of canals stretches for 600 miles (965 km). The biggest canals were closest to the rivers and were up to 64 feet (19.5 meters) wide. As the canals branched off into different channels, they grew narrower. Canals only 6 feet (1.8 meters) across, where people could easily get water, ran through villages.

What did they eat?

The canals not only watered the crops; they also carried small particles of soil and sand from the rivers. These particles settled as silt. Silt carried more nutrients than the sandy desert soil, so it helped more plants grow.

The Hohokam cultivated maize (corn), beans, and squash. Throughout the region archaeologists have found smooth, basin-shaped hollows ground into rocks. The Hohokam used them as mortars, or bowls, in which to grind beans from the mesquite tree. That produced a sweet, nutty-tasting flour that could be eaten on its own or mixed with other foods or with drinks. Mesquite could also be eaten without being cooked.

Archaeologists have learned what other plants grew in the region. They analyze pollen, tiny particles that plants use to reproduce. Most vegetable matter rots over a long time, but pollen sometimes survives. It is different for every plant, so it reveals exactly what grew where.

Pollen shows that the Hohokam diet likely included wild plants such as mustard, buckwheat, and cactuses. After they had eaten the organ-pipe cactus once, the Hohokam dried their waste and cleaned the seeds that had not been digested. They could then eat them again and make sure that the seeds were chewed open.

Snaketown

Before the 1930s, no one realized that the Hohokam were a separate group. Two men were responsible for telling them apart them from the other Southwestern cultures. One was Harold S. Gladwin, who founded the Gila Pueblo Archaeological Foundation. The other was the man who has been called the most important archaeologist of the Southwest, Emil W. Haury.

In 1937 Gladwin and Haury published a study of a site known as

< The seeds of the organ-pipe cactus were so full of protein that the Hohokam learned to eat them twice.

Playing hardball

At Snaketown Gladwin and Haury found large courts dug into the ground. They believed the courts were used by the Hohokam to play a variation of a sacred game played by the Maya of southern Mexico. Ball courts throughout Mesoamerica indicate that the game was also played by many other peoples. Carvings show that the game involved using the elbows and knees to pass a small rubber ball through iron rings set high on the sides of the court.

Just building a court would have taken a lot of labor, so the ball game may have had a religious importance. In cultures such as the Maya and Olmec—though likely not among the Hohokam—players were sacrificed to the gods. Experts are not sure, however, whether it was the losing team who died, or the winners.

Snaketown. It was named for the O'Odham word Shoaquick, which means "Place of the Snakes." The site covered 250 acres (100 ha) on the north bank of the Gila River, 30 miles (48 km) upstream from its junction with the Salt River.

The archaeologists found around 40 houses, two ball courts, and a canal. There were also flat-topped mounds and the remains of 500 cremations. Thirty years later Haury returned and found more houses, another ballcourt, and more cremations.

▼ **Pieces of broken pottery still lie scattered on the ground at Snaketown. At its height, the site may have been home to up to a thousand people.**

Each dwelling at Snaketown stood for around 25 years, after which a new home was built on the ruins of the first. The houses were built in foot-deep pits and had posts to support roofs made from brush that kept out the sun's heat. The sides were covered with clay.

Haury used radiocarbon dating to learn more about Snaketown. All living things contain traces of the element carbon. When they die, it begins to decay at a steady rate. By measuring how much carbon has decayed, it is possible to tell when an animal, person, plant, or tree died. The technique allows archaeologists to tell, for example, when a tree was cut down to provide wood for building.

A big house

The most impressive Hohokam ruin is Casa Grande, or Big House, which stands between the Gila and Santa Cruz rivers. Archaeologists believe that it was one of a number of settlements linked by canals. The four-story building was made from caliche, a natural material formed of mineral particles cemented together with lime.

▽ The ruins of the main building at Casa Grande stand beneath a canopy built by archaeologists to protect it from the effects of the sun and the rain.

This artist's re-creation shows one version of what might have become of the Hohokam. It shows them moving out of the Salt River Valley after they had lost control of the water supply and could no longer survive in the desert.

The caliche has survived the desert temperatures for over 600 years.

The purpose of Casa Grande is still a mystery. Steven Shackley believes that it may have been a home for the elite members of Hohokam society. Another theory is that it was used for studying the stars. The upper story has a round opening. On the summer solstice, the longest day of the year, the edges of the opening line up with the setting sun. That would tell the Hohokam when summer started changing to fall and harvest time was getting near.

Changing theories

Evidence shows that the Hohokam had close contacts with Mesoamerica. The ball game they played, like the flat-topped mounds they built, was shared by cultures farther south, such as the Maya. Their language was related to Nahuatl, the language of the Aztec. Emil Haury even suggested that the Hohokam had come from Mexico. Few people now believe that theory—the Hohokam were more likely influenced by Mesoamericans through trade and other contact with them. But Steven Shackley's little pieces of obsidian may still have much to reveal about the connections between the Hohokam and their neighbors.

The Ancient Ones

Who lived in the great Cliff Palace?

On a sunny day in 1929 Charles Lindbergh took the archaeologist Alfred V. Kidder for a flight in his propeller plane. Lindbergh had become a hero for being the first person to fly across the Atlantic from the United States to Europe. Now he was helping Kidder survey ruins in the deserts of New Mexico. They made many flights together. Today's destination was one of the most spectacular ancient sites, Chaco Canyon, once occupied by the Anasazi. Kidder used

< The Cliff Palace at Mesa Verde is hidden away and easy to defend—yet there is little sign that its builders faced any great danger from possible attackers.

ANASAZI
ca A.D. 100 – 1600

| 0 | A.D. 1000 | A.D. 2000 |

a camera to photograph the site for the first time from above. He could get a revealing view of ancient sites from the air.

The 10-mile-long (16 km) canyon was scattered with ruins. There were the remains of large buildings that experts named "great houses." Most archaeologists believe that the buildings may have been used for rituals, although some think they may have been homes for the elite. There were also multistory dwellings built into cliffs, like apartment buildings. Kidder and others suggested that the whole canyon was likely a ritual and

∧ Pueblo Bonito's giant D-shape covered three acres (1 ha). Although it took the Anasazi 200 years to build the pueblo, it all seems to have been planned from the start. Roads led to the site from many smaller communities, so it was likely an important center.

political center for the farmers who lived in the region that is now called Four Corners.

A central canyon

The Anasazi were farmers who for centuries left traces of settlement throughout northwestern New Mexico. They traded objects such as beads as far as the Pacific and Gulf coasts of Mexico. They grew squash, corn, and beans for food, and cotton for making cloth. They hunted animals to add meat to their diet.

It was a struggle to get food in the dry environment, and the early Anasazi seem to have moved around. Some experts think that they found new places to settle as areas became unsuitable for farming, perhaps after a river changed course or dried up.

The basketmakers

The early Anasazi were skilled basketmakers. They used the stems of willow and other plants to weave baskets and sandals. Their designs got more complex over the centuries. Experts use this changing basketwork

Dating system

Most archaeologists use an approximate system of dating the Pueblo based on changing styles of settlements and artifacts:

ARCHAIC (6500 B.C.–A.D. 1) This period came before the emergence of the Pueblo

BASKETMAKER II (A.D. 1–500) Semi-nomadic people lived by hunting and gathering food

BASKETMAKER III (500–700) As agriculture increased, communities became more settled

PUEBLO I (700–900) People lived in communities of adjoining rooms and used underground kivas for ceremonies

PUEBLO II (900–1150) Settlements and kivas became more diverse

PUEBLO III (1150–1300) The great cliff dwellings were built

PUEBLO IV (1300–1600) The Anasazi moved south and east to begin new communities

PUEBLO V (1600–present) Modern Pueblo peoples live in the Southwest

V This artist's reconstruction shows a hunter returning to Pueblo Bonito as it may have looked at its most powerful.

to date different groups of early Anasazi. However, the people seem to have stopped making so many baskets after the sixth century. Archaeologists believe that was when the Anasazi learned how to make vessels from pottery.

Checking out Chaco

Chaco Canyon was first discovered by non-native peoples in the 1850s, when it was found by a military survey. It was so remote from where most Americans lived, however, that it was only late in the 1800s that the work of a cowboy named Richard Wetherill made the site well known. The people who lived there seem to have been a distinct group. Archaeologists have given them the name Chaco.

< The bands on this artwork show stages in the development of the Anasazi. From nomadic hunters (far left), they became settled farmers growing corn. In the third band, the basketmakers have moved into cliff bulidings. The final band shows the Classic age, when the Anasazi made fine pottery and used underground kivas for religious ceremonies.

The rise and fall of the Chaco is one of the great mysteries of the Southwest. In 1920, the National Geographic Society began excavating the settlement known as Pueblo Bonito ("Beautiful Village"). Their work was taken over by the National Museum of American History, which conducted a preliminary survey of the "apartment house" at the site.

The curious cowboy

Cowboy and rancher Richard Wetherill was a leading figure in the growth of archaeology in the Southwest. His discovery of the Cliff Palace of Mesa Verde on December 18, 1888, made him famous. But although Wetherill liked to explore old sites, he did not care much about preserving them or learning about the past. He and his brothers were more interested in selling the objects they found, something that shocks modern archaeologists. The Wetherills turned their ranch into a guesthouse for tourists and showed them the ruins. In 1896 Wetherill joined excavations by the National Museum of American History at Pueblo Bonito in Chaco Canyon.

Wetherill also tried to establish a homestead in the canyon, claiming land that included Pueblo Bonito, Pueblo del Arroyo, and Chetro Ketl. In 1907, he was forced to give up his claim when President Theodore Roosevelt made the canyon a national monument.

∧ Richard Wetherill (*right*) and his brother John pause for lunch while searching for artifacts at Spruce Tree House, Mesa Verde, which Richard discovered in December 1888.

The dwelling was shaped like a large semicircle, with a flat front wall and a curved back. The five-story building may have been home to as many as 1,200 people. They lived in a network of 600 to 800 interconnected rooms, like many houses joined together. The pueblo is also home to 36 roofed pits called kivas, which were used for religious ceremonies.

Construction started around A.D. 900 and continued over the next two centuries, but experts studying the ruins believe that the whole building was planned from the start. The walls were made from sandstone blocks cemented with mortar, a building technique unique to Chaco Canyon.

Stephen Lekson believes that Pueblo Bonito was built by the Chaco leaders as an expression of their power. He argues that they intended it to impress visitors from other communities. Not everyone agrees; many experts believe that the Anasazi had no formal leaders but were guided by senior members of the community.

A mystery remains

On the remote northern rim of Chaco Canyon stand the ruins of Pueblo Alto.

Excavations there began in 1976—and they raised more questions than they answered. The pueblo is different from the other settlements in the canyon. It has some 85 rooms, but there is little evidence that most of them were used to live in. Experts found numerous pieces of broken pottery: more than 70,000. But there was no way the number of people who could have lived in the pueblo could have generated so much trash. The math didn't work.

One theory is that perhaps the site was used for gatherings of groups scattered in and around Chaco Canyon. The great houses that dot the canyon have often been thought of as ritual centers for different groups. Perhaps Pueblo Alto played a role in bringing all the Anasazi groups together. Roads that run for miles across the desert meet at the site.

The sun dagger

To descendants of the Pueblo, Chaco Canyon is a sacred site. Evidence of the special role it had for their ancestors lies hidden near the top of a rock outcrop called Fajada Butte— home to the so-called Sun Dagger.

Near the top of the butte three slabs of rock lie vertically across the face of a large niche. The slabs do not touch, leaving two thin gaps between them through which the sun lights up the niche at about midday. Inside the niche, the Chaco carved two spirals. Experts studying the designs in 1977

∧ The dry heat of the Southwest has preserved Anasazi remains for over 800 years, including this woven sandal. The climate has also preserved some Anasazi bodies, which were placed in caves. They dried out and became mummies.

Southwestern spirits

One element shared by the Pueblo cultures was the kiva. Although they came in various shapes and sizes at different times and in different places, they all shared the same purpose. They were used for religious and ritual gatherings. After the 12th century, kivas were at the heart of every Pueblo settlement—and they remain at the heart of native communities in the Southwest.

For the modern Hopi and Zuni, the kiva marks a place where the living can come into contact with the spirits of their ancestors. The ancient kivas likely had a similar purpose. In the middle of the floor was a hole or indentation called a *sipapu*. It symbolized the connection between the two worlds.

The earliest kivas were round pits dug into the ground and lined with stone walls. They were often roofed with logs, and had a trapdoor and ladder that allowed access to the inside and a hole to let out smoke from the fires burning inside. As the Pueblo cultures developed, so kivas became more elaborate. After about A.D. 1100, they were increasingly larger—like the Anasazi Great Kiva at Mesa Verde—or built above ground in a variety of shapes.

One useful way to date kivas is to study magnetism. The Earth's magnetic field moves over time. When clay is heated, magnetic particles within it become aligned with the Earth's magnetic field at the time. By comparing the clay surrounding the fireplaces in the kivas with the record of the Earth's magnetic field, experts can discover approximately when a fire was last lit in the hearth.

∧ **This reconstruction at Aztec Ruins National Monument in New Mexico shows common features of a Great Kiva, including a stone bench along the wall, rectangular fireplaces dug into the ground, and a square sipapu. This kiva was built above ground, with windows and a skylight for illumination.**

noticed that at the summer solstice—the longest day in the year—a dagger of sunlight falls exactly across the middle of the larger spiral. At the winter solstice, the shortest day of the year, two daggers of light fall precisely on opposite outer edges of the larger spiral. At the spring and fall equinoxes, on the other hand, when day and night are equal length, the light daggers fall across both the spirals.

The Sun Dagger seems to be a calendar that marks the cycle of the sun throughout the year. Experts

∧ Fajada Butte was just one of a number of natural features around Chaco Canyon the Chaco used to follow the movement of the sun throughout the year.

➤ This artist's re-creation shows a shaman performing a ritual in an underground kiva of the Rio Grande Anasazi.

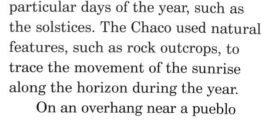

∧ This painted headdress may have been worn during ceremonies that appealed to ancestor spirits called kachinas to look after a community.

studying the slabs believe that they were not put in place by the Chaco, but fell there naturally. The Chaco must have noticed that the dagger acted as a natural "clock" and carved the spirals to chart the sun's progress. That allowed them to study the changes of the seasons. The dry Southwest was a tough place to grow anything, so it was vital for farmers to know when to plant or harvest their crops.

Sky watchers

Astronomy seems to have been vital in Chaco life. Experts have found that 11 of the major buildings in Chaco Canyon were oriented to face the sun or the moon on particular days of the year, such as the solstices. The Chaco used natural features, such as rock outcrops, to trace the movement of the sunrise along the horizon during the year.

On an overhang near a pueblo named Penasco Blanco there appears what may be even more remarkable evidence of the Chaco interest in astronomy. A pictograph shows a hand, a crescent moon, a star, and a dot surrounded by three concentric circles, which may be intended to represent the sun.

The site was found in the early 1970s. Ray A. Williamson, an archaeologist who specializes in astronomy, argued that

∧ A woman performs a dance to bring rain in this painting from Pueblo Bonito. Rain was precious: Drought was a constant threat in the dry environment.

Space-age views of the past

In 1984 jets from the National Aeronautical and Space Administration (NASA) roared over Chaco Canyon. They were carrying out a survey using infrared scanners. It was the same technology NASA used to study the surface of the moon. The scanners produce images based on heat. The images are colored to show patterns that are invisible to the naked eye.

The NASA images of Chaco Canyon revealed a series of lines running straight across the desert. The lines were roads. They showed up as a different color because the earth in them had been packed tight, so it kept more heat than the loose earth all around.

The roads extended hundreds of miles into Chaco territory in what are now Utah and southwestern Colorado. But the Anasazi had no wheeled vehicles, so why did they build roads as wide as 30 feet (9 meters)? One theory is that the roads did not only have a practical purpose but were also sacred paths, connected to rituals. Another theory is that the roads connected up to 150 outlying settlements to Chaco, at the heart of the territory.

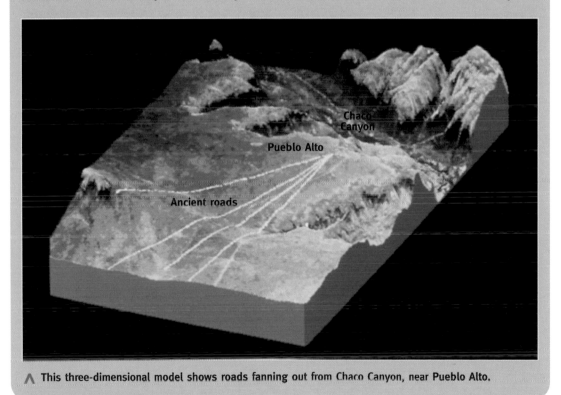

Λ **This three-dimensional model shows roads fanning out from Chaco Canyon, near Pueblo Alto.**

the images represent a real event. On July 4, 1054, a star died in a huge explosion called a supernova. The light from the supernova was visible for three weeks. Astronomers recorded the event around the world. Williamson believes that the Chaco recorded their own image of the supernova.

A controversial theory

Why did the Anasazi leave Chaco Canyon? One theory was put forward by Stephen Lekson in 1999. He suggested that Chaco's leaders deliberately moved the community. Lekson had his idea when he noticed that Chaco Canyon lined up on a north–south axis with two other ancient sites. First, he says, in about 1125 the Chaco headed 50 miles (80 km) north to a place now named Aztec Ruins. Nearly two hundred years later, they moved again—this time 450 miles (720 km) due south to what is now Paquimé in Mexico. Lekson argues that archaeological evidence connects all three sites. Other scholars profoundly disagree.

Lekson also supports an even more controversial theory. When problems affected Chaco Canyon after about 1100, he believes, life became more nasty and violent. Christy G. Turner, an archaeologist at Arizona State University, has examined human bones found throughout the Southwest. He believes he has found signs of cannibalism, or eating human flesh. In Lekson's view, the Chaco leaders staged displays of ritual cannibalism to assert their own power and make sure that everyone recognized it.

The greatest mystery

Archaeologists think that there was a golden age at Chaco Canyon between 1030 and 1125. Soon after, however, the site was abandoned for nearly a thousand years. Why that might have happened remains a mystery. Some experts think that a drought may have made it impossible to grow crops.

Another theory is that a power struggle between the rulers of Chaco led the people to move on.

Mesa Verde

The end of Chaco Canyon was not the end of the Anasazi, however. They survived at sites such as Mesa Verde in Colorado. This "green table"—a flat-topped mountain named by Spanish explorers for the trees on the summit—is home to some 600 ancient sites. Some are high on cliffs that are now almost inaccessible. The ancient residents probably climbed to them using rope ladders or footholds carved into the rock. Experts still find new sites throughout the Southwest. High on cliffs, they are almost impossible to spot from the ground.

Mesa Verde is home to one of the Anasazi's most remarkable monuments. Discovered by Richard Wetherill in 1888, the Cliff Palace is named for its multi-storied tower. Nestled beneath a rock ledge was a mini-city of 151 rooms and 23 kivas.

V **This Anasazi pot was used for storing seeds. It was dug up at Cortez, in Colorado, near Mesa Verde.**

The structures provided room for living, storing supplies, and practicing rituals. Wetherill found many artifacts, including pottery, axes, and sandals made from yucca leaves.

The Mesa Verde buildings were much smaller than those at Chaco Canyon. The rooms were so low that the inhabitants would not have been able to stand up easily. The doors were small to keep out the winter winds. As in Chaco Canyon, their kivas had wall benches, vents, fire pits, and other pits dug into the floor. Unlike the circular kivas at Chaco, however, some at Mesa Verde were square or rectangular.

Moving on

After barely a century, the Anasazi abandoned Mesa Verde—and the whole Four Corners region. Evidence

▽ Potter Clint Swink (*right*) burns wood in a trench as he re-creates an Anasazi kiln for firing pottery. It took him six years to perfect the technique.

from tree rings shows that there was a major drought shortly before. However, sites were still being built at Mesa Verde during the 20-year drought, so the drought probably did not force out the Anasazi on its own.

The drop in rainfall may have combined with other factors, such as an increase in population. Some experts claim that evidence of outbreaks of violence show that society was breaking down at this time. Food shortages drove small groups away from the great site to smaller settlements. They became the forebears of the modern Pueblo people, such as the Hopi and Zuni.

The Master Potters

CHAPTER 4

Who were the Mogollon?

In 1914 Jesse Fewkes of the Smithsonian Institution in Washington D.C. boarded a train for New Mexico. The journey took days, but Fewkes, who was an expert on Native Americans, had received an interesting letter from an amateur archaeologist. E. D. Osborn had written Fewkes about several hundred painted pots discovered in burial sites on his family's ranch. When Fewkes arrived in New Mexico, he was amazed by the variety and quality of the pots on the Osborn ranch. He was

< Designs scratched into a rock likely had a spiritual meaning for the Mogollon— but they remain an intriguing mystery for modern researchers.

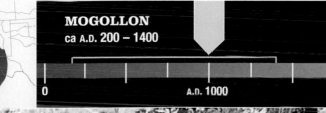

MOGOLLON
ca A.D. 200 – 1400

0 A.D. 1000 A.D. 2000

so determined to find out about the people who had created such beautiful objects that he devoted 20 years to learning about them.

A new group?

The potters were a people archaeologists call the Mimbres, who had lived in southwestern New Mexico. To begin with, most experts assumed that the Mimbres were part of the Anasazi. That changed in the mid-1930s. Archaeologist Emil Haury, who had previously identified the Hohokam, now suggested that the Mimbres were part of a separate cultural group. This was, he argued, a third group of Pueblo. They lived in the mountains of Arizona and New Mexico, higher above sea level than their Hohokam neighbors.

Marvelous Mimbres

The pottery of the Mimbres people, who lived in the Southern Gila Wilderness for almost one thousand years (200–1150), is the most striking physical record of the Mogollon civilization.

We know that the pottery was made by women because pottery-making tools have turned up in burial sites, but only with female bodies. By about 700, the Mimbres pots had begun to feature complex and beautiful designs. Archaeologists often call Mimbres pottery "black-on-white," but that is misleading. Depending on the temperature at which it was fired, its colors could vary from orange to black.

The pots were decorated with animals, birds, and human figures. Some drawings show real

∧ **The figures on this Mimbres bowl may be a man and woman, or symbols of life and death.**

creatures, such as quail, in such detail that it is still possible to identify them. Experts have identified other figures as characters from the myths of the Aztec, who lived in what is now central Mexico. They include the plumed serpent, Quetzalcoatl, and the rain god, Tlaloc. Such evidence suggests that there was extensive communication between the civilizations.

Mimbres pottery often had a ritual purpose. Pots were buried in graves—but only after having had a round hole made in them (*above*). This "breaking" of the pot may have been done to release the spirit after death.

∧ Jesse Fewkes stands beside a collection of artifacts—and bones—from Mesa Verde in 1918. The cabin was originally a ranger station, but was converted into the first museum at the site—and the first opened anywhere by the National Park Service.

Early and late

Haury named the people the Mogollon for one of the mountain ranges in New Mexico, near the San Francisco River. More than other Southwestern peoples, he argued, the Mogollon had relied on hunting and gathering plants rather than farming. The Mogollon was an early culture, he said, but later they merged with the Anasazi. The two had eventually become impossible to tell apart.

Haury's theory was one of the most controversial ideas in American archaeology for much of the 1940s. Many archaeologists simply refused to acknowledge the Mogollon as being separate from the Anasazi. By the late 1960s evidence from artifacts and sites had convinced most experts, but even today some do not believe that the Mogollon were a distinct group.

Rings within rings

In 1944 Haury studied tree rings from Bluff Village, a site in the Forestdale Valley. He learned that the Mogollon had lived there as early as A.D. 300. More recent advances in dendrochronology have pushed back the date of the appearance of the Mogollon at least another hundred years to around A.D. 200.

< Mogollon hunters used sharp flint points for their arrows and spears; these were found near Truth or Consequences in New Mexico.

size. None of the burial pits in which the Mogollon placed their dead were more extravagant than another.

LeBlanc's research supported earlier views of the Ancestral Pueblo as having been very equal societies. Since the 1970s, however, more experts have challenged that theory. They believe that it represents an idealized vision of these Native American peoples.

By the 11th century, the Mogollon had moved from their scattered villages to larger settlements. Their pit houses were replaced by multiroom houses. Archaeologists think that beginning about this time the Mogollon were living closely with their neighbors, the Anasazi, and may have absorbed influences from them. As Mogollon sites became larger, they irrigated fields and grew more crops.

An equal society

In the 1970s the archaeologist Steven LeBlanc made another important breakthrough in understanding the Mogollon. LeBlanc determined from studies of Mogollon villages that there was no evidence that society was divided into different ranks. Everyone was treated as an equal. There seem to have been no rulers and no class of nobles. All the houses were of a similar

> This petroglyph showing a bighorn sheep struck by arrows is a reminder of the importance of hunting to the Mogollon.

∧ The forested Mogollon Mountains in New Mexico gave the Ancestral Pueblo who lived there their modern name.

Grasshopper Pueblo

The change in Mogollon culture was marked by the rapid growth of Grasshopper Pueblo in the mountains of east-central Arizona. Within only thirty years the pueblo became a substantial settlement.

Grasshopper Pueblo was located in the middle of the Mogollon's largest area of agricultural land. The pueblo was made up of 500 rooms divided into three distinct areas with three plazas. Unlike earlier Mogollon settlements of pit houses dug into the ground, it had free-standing homes with masonry walls one or two stories tall.

One of the plazas was roofed over and transformed into a large kiva

Bone breakthrough

In the late 1980s new data about Grasshopper Pueblo came from experts at the University of Wisconsin in Madison. They analyzed human remains from the site for forms of the element strontium. Strontium occurs in most rocks but in different forms that can be traced to specific regions. Humans absorb tiny amounts of strontium in water and food. It builds up in their teeth and bones. The strontium in teeth does not change, so it shows where people spent their childhood, when their teeth were forming. The strontium in bones changes as people age, so it reveals where they spent the last part of their lives. At Grasshopper Pueblo, half the people whose remains were analyzed had grown up far away, perhaps to the north. That supported the idea that the pueblo had taken in migrants, maybe from other cultures.

∧ Mogollon artifacts made from animal bones. They include awls (*right*) used to pierce animal skins to stitch them together.

where communal events could be held. Other parts of the pueblo had smaller kivas, which were probably shared by related family groups.

Grasshopper Pueblo grew steadily for thirty years. Its growth reflected a period of higher than average rainfall that allowed the inhabitants to grow more crops. It also reflected the arrival of new residents. Some of the new arrivals, experts believe, may have been Anasazi moving away from the Colorado Plateau.

In about 1330, however, the rains started to fail. The region grew drier. The soil had few nutrients left, and farmers could no longer feed the population. Analysis of bones found in burial sites at Grasshopper shows that the people had begun to suffer from diseases associated with a lack of proper nutrition.

What happened to the Mogollon?

The Mogollon abandoned settlements at Grasshopper, Forestdale, and Point of Pines in the mountains of Arizona at about the same time. Archaeologists studying their disappearance wonder if that might mean that what happened at Grasshopper may have been repeated at the other sites—a larger population and a lack of food forced the inhabitants to move.

It is impossible to follow the Mogollon tracks, however. By about

1400 they had merged with the Anasazi to such an extent that, even using the most modern techniques, archaeologists cannot distinguish the two groups. It may be that the Mogollon simply faded away, or were absorbed by the more powerful group.

Past and present

Archaeologists are fairly certain that descendants of the Mogollon live today among the Native Americans of the Southwest. For modern Pueblo, there is no question about what became of the Mogollon—or the Hohokam or the Anasazi. They may have moved from their former centers of population, but they still lived in sizable settlements throughout the region. Their descendants today sometimes live in multiroomed pueblo houses that echo those built by their ancestors.

The imposing ancient sites, however, were abandoned. By the time the Spanish explorer Francisco Vásquez de Coronado reached the mountains of central Arizona in 1540, he found the ancient ruins empty of people—but still full of the signs of the past.

▽ A Mogollon cliff dwelling at Gila Cliff stands behind an edible prickly pear cactus; cactus fruit was part of the early Mogollon's diet.

Meet an Archaeologist

Stephen Lekson of the University of Colorado has been studying sites throughout the Southwest for more than 20 years. He is one of the leading experts on Chaco Canyon and the Chaco.

◙ What made you want to be an archaelogist?
▣ When I was in high school, my family lived in Naples, Italy, and we often visited the ancient Roman ruins at Pompeii. That "hooked" me.

◙ When did you get interested in the Southwest?
▣ My first archaeological experience was on a "field school" in New Mexico. The archaeology was great, but mostly I was very impressed with the night sky. I'd never seen the Milky Way, and there it was! There were so many stars!

◙ What's the best part of your job?
▣ Working in the field:
finding sites, mapping, excavating. And working with students and young archaeologists.

◙ What's the worst part of your job?
▣ Working in the office: committee meetings, financial statements, appointments.

◙ What are the most important qualities for an archaeologist?
▣ Puzzle-solving, patience, good humor. Archaeology is not a job for hasty, crabby people.

◙ What was the most important discovery you've ever made?
▣ Finding a big Mesa Verde
town 250 miles (400 km) south of Mesa Verde. We weren't expecting to find it, but there it was.

◙ What are the biggest challenges for working in the Southwest?
▣ Realizing that the spectacular cliff dwellings of Mesa Verde were only a small part of the picture. And recognizing that distances we find daunting, they didn't. A few hundred miles was not a big deal for migration or pilgrimage or trading.

◙ Do you have any advice for children who want to become archaeologists?
▣ Study math and science and writing. Spend lots of

time outdoors, exploring. Archaeology is fun because you spend a lot of time outside, using your head.

◻ What techniques have been most useful for your work in the Southwest?

◻ Geometry, for making good maps and drawings. Map-reading, for not getting lost. And writing: It's vital to write clearly, and it helps to write well—which are two different things.

◻ Were the Hohokam, the Anasazi, and the Mogollon so very different from one another?

◻ The Hohokam and the Anasazi were indeed very different: different languages, economies, houses, and habits. "Mogollon" is an archaeological term for the area in between Anasazi and Hohokam; and the more we learn about the Mogollon area, the less "real" (or independent) it becomes.

◻ Why do you think the Pueblo peoples left their ancient homes?

◻ A combination of reasons: political declines, over-crowding, droughts, and warfare all played roles. But Pueblo people will tell you that the reasons for moving from one place to another were usually spiritual. People were not living correctly, and their priests and spiritual

∧ Stephen Lekson (*center*) and his wife, archaeologist Catherine Cameron (*left*), examine ruins with a colleague at Bluff Great House in southeastern Utah.

advisers would tell them to move on. In their migrations, they learned how to live properly as Pueblo people. Leaving an old village and founding a new village were ways of learning.

◻ Can we learn anything about the ancient Peublo from their modern descendants?

◻ Modern Pueblo people remember, in great detail, their histories and migrations. Archaeologists can learn a lot about the past from Pueblo migration stories. On the other hand, things in the past were very different, so archaeologists can't rely on modern Pueblo life as a

model for what happened, for example, in Chaco Canyon. Just as we can't look at New York City today and assume that New York in 1700 was the same. The past was different.

◻ What question would you most like to answer about the ancient Pueblo?

◻ How much they knew about the Mississippi Valley. We know that the Pueblo knew all about Mesoamerica, but at the same time the Mississippi Valley, from St Louis to New Orleans, was filled with big cities. Pueblo people were great traders and explorers, and the Mississippi people were, too: How much did they know about each other?

Back to the Future

CHAPTER 5

How can we care for Pueblo sites?

Americans love to travel—and many visit the sites of the Ancestral Pueblo. Almost as soon as they were discovered, places such as Mesa Verde faced problems caused by the number of visitors. In 1893, Richard Wetherill put a scale model of the cliff houses at Mesa Verde on show at the Columbian Exposition in Chicago. It was seen by 12 million people. Visitors flocked to Colorado to see for themselves. The Wetherill brothers turned their ranch into a guesthouse for some of the first tourists to visit the region. By the middle of the 1890s, the area was crowded with

< A Pueblo girl wears a traditional costume to take part in a corn dance, which is performed to encourage a good crop.

visitors. At the time the ancient sites had no protection. People took anything they liked.

In 1906, Virginia McClurg and Lucy Peabody began to urge the government to protect Mesa Verde. Thanks to their efforts, it was made a national monument, which celebrated its 100th anniversary in 2006.

Number puzzle

Mesa Verde is the most visited archaeological site in the United States. About 800,000 visitors a year have the chance to find out more about the Ancestral Pueblo. But all those people threaten the site. Scientists now know that even the breath of so many tourists may damage the ancient remains. They have survived so well for centuries because the air is perfectly dry—but people's breath contains moisture that makes the air damp. Tourists can no longer climb inside kivas or other structures because the sandstone has become too crumbly. The National Park Service tries to strike a balance between allowing the public to visit America's heritage and protecting precious sites for serious study.

∧ A sign of continuity: Modern Pueblo craftspeople still make turquoise jewelry like that of their ancestors.

Pushing and pulling

Some questions about the Pueblo come up time and time again. The biggest is why they abandoned their spectacular centers. Previous theories often asked what might have driven them away. Now experts also wonder whether there was a "pull" as well as a "push." Did something attract the Pueblo to new regions?

A theory put forward by Anasazi scholar Bill Lipe is that a new religion had developed to the south and east of the Colorado Plateau. It appealed to ancestor spirits—kachinas—to look after the community. The religion began in about the 13th century and is still practiced. Lipe believes that the Anasazi may have moved to join the new faith. Other scholars argue that the timing is wrong: By the time the religion appeared, the Anasazi had already abandoned the Colorado Plateau.

Surviving culture

More clues about the Ancestral Pueblo come from their descendants. The Jemez, for example, live 40 miles (60 km) outside Albuquerque in New Mexico. They tell how their ancestors left the Colorado Plateau and traveled hundreds of miles to a mesa where they built a 2,300-room pueblo named Kwanstiyukwa, "place of the pine bird." The village was bigger than any built by the Anasazi. Its ruins still look out over today's smaller pueblo. For the Jemez and other peoples of the Southwest, the "Ancient Ones" are still part of modern life.

▽ Without even realizing it, visitors to sites such as Mesa Verde can damage the very treasures they have come to see.

The Years Ahead

In little more than a decade, the Cliff Palace at Mesa Verde went from being a treasure-house of artifacts for visitors to take to being a protected national monument. But that short period cost archaeologists many valuable clues about the past. Today, however, new sites are still being discovered in the Southwest that may offer new clues.

Universities in the region are in the forefront of the search. They have benefited from the fact that more people are living in the Southwest and have brought increased prosperity. The universities have money to attract top archaeologists to study the region's past. They are seeking to fill in some of the blanks in the record. How close were Anasazi connections with the cultures of Mexico, for example? And did the Mogollon really live in a society without rulers or classes?

Meanwhile, there is a new generation of Native American archaeologists who claim descent from the Pueblo. They are looking again at the lives of their ancestors and highlighting the shared elements between their own lives and those of the past. They do not ask what happened to the ancient Pueblo. For them, the answer is clear: "We're still here, and we've been here all along."

∧ Candles light up the Cliff Palace during a celebration at Mesa Verde.

Glossary

abstract – describes a design that does not represent something real, such as a person or object

ancestors – the previous generations of a family

artifact – any object changed by human activity

butte – a hill or mountain with a flat top and steep sides

canal – an artificial waterway

canopy – a covering fixed above an object or place

canyon – a narrow river valley with steep sides

ceramics – objects made from clay

circa – about; used to indicate a date that is approximate, and abbreviated as ca

cremation – the burning of a dead body

drought – a long period of low rainfall

ethnic – relating to a group that has a shared background

excavation – an archaeological dig

flint – a type of hard rock that was used by ancient peoples for blades and to strike to make sparks for starting fires

great house – a multiroomed, multistoried building constructed by the Ancestral Pueblo. No one is sure what the great houses were used for.

irrigation – any human-made system for carrying water to farmland

mesa – a broad, flat-topped area of land with steep sides

Mesoamerica – Middle America; a term used to describe an area from central Mexico south through Guatemala, Belize, Honduras, and El Salvador

mesquite – a spiny shrub that grows throughout the Southwest; its seedpods are eaten by animals and humans

mortar – a smooth, hard bowl used for grinding food, often with a tool called a pestle

mummies – dead bodies that are preserved by being dried out

niche – a small hollow in a wall, usually for holding an object or objects

nutrient – a substance in food that plants or animals need to live

petroglyph – an ancient carving on a rock

pit houses – homes that are partially dug into the ground

plaza – an open area in a town or other settlement

pollen – tiny particles the size of dust that are used by plants for reproduction

pottery – artifacts made from clay, such as pots and plates

rituals – repeated practices, often religious

Shaman – a priest or priestess

stratigraphy – the study of different layers, or strata, of remains in the ground

supernova – the explosion of a star

survey – a careful collection of data about an area or subject

theory – in science, the explanation that best fits the available evidence

yucca – a plant with long, stiff, sword-shaped leaves

Bibliography

Books

Mound Builders and Cliff Dwellers (Lost Civilizations series). Alexandria, VA: Time-Life Books, 1992.

Gibbon, Guy E. *Archaeology of Prehistoric Native America: An Encyclopedia*. New York: Routledge, 1998.

Articles

Arnold, David L. "Pueblo Pottery: 2,000 Years of Artistry." NATIONAL GEOGRAPHIC (November 1982): 593–605.

Creamer, Winifred, and Jonathan Haas. "Pueblo: Search for the Ancient Ones." NATIONAL GEOGRAPHIC (October 1996): 84–99.

Roberts, David. "The Old Ones of the Southwest." NATIONAL GEOGRAPHIC (April 1996): 86–109.

Roberts, David. "Stephen Lekson Has a Theory." NG ADVENTURE. (March 2005): 50–57, 87.

Further Reading

Larson, Timothy. *Anasazi* (Ancient Civilizations). Austin, TX: Steadwell Books, 2001.

St. Lawrence, Genevieve. *The Pueblo and their History* (We the People). Minneapolis, MN: Compass Point Books, 2005.

Stuart, George E. *Ancient Pioneers: The First Americans*. Washington, D.C.: National Geographic, 2001.

On the Web

Ancient Observatories Chaco Canyon Site
http://www.exploratorium.edu/chaco/

Chaco Digital Initiative
http://www.chacoarchive.org/index.html

National Park Service, Aztec Ruins National Monument
http://www.nps.gov/azru

National Park Service, Chaco Culture National Historical Park
http://www.nps.gov/chcu/

National Park Service, Mesa Verde National Park
http://www.nps.gov/meve/

Index

About the Author

ANITA CROY has written many books for children, mainly about geography and history. She holds a doctorate in Latin American studies from the University of London. Since she married a native of Colorado, she has spent part of each year exploring the American Southwest. She looks forward to the time when she can watch her young son climb ladders at Pueblo sites without worrying that he's about to fall.

About the Consultant

J. JEFFERSON REID is a professor of anthropology at the University of Arizona. In over forty seasons of fieldwork, he has excavated sites throughout the Southwest and Mesoamerica, as well as in the southeastern United States. He led excavations at the Mogollon site at Grasshopper Pueblo throughout the 1980s and was formerly editor of *American Antiquity*, the journal of the Society for American Archaeology.

> A kachina doll made by modern descendants of the Pueblo

One of the world's largest nonprofit
scientific and educational organizations, the
National Geographic Society was founded in
1888 "for the increase and diffusion of
geographic knowledge." Fulfilling this
mission, the Society educates and inspires millions
every day through its magazines, books, television
programs, videos, maps and atlases, research grants,
the National Geographic Bee, teacher workshops, and
innovative classroom materials. The Society is
supported through membership dues, charitable gifts,
and income from the sale of its educational products.
This support is vital to National Geographic's mission
to increase global understanding and promote
conservation of our planet through exploration,
research, and education.

For more information, please call 1-800-NGS-LINE
(647-5463) or write to the following address:

National Geographic Society
1145 17th Street N.W.
Washington, D.C. 20036-4688
U.S.A.

Visit the Society's Web site:
www.nationalgeographic.com

Library of Congress Cataloging-in-Publication Data
available upon request
Hardcover ISBN: 978-1-4263-0130-8
Library Edition ISBN: 978-1-4263-0131-5

Printed in Mexico

Series design by Jim Hiscott
The body text is set in Century Schoolbook
The display text is set in Helvetica Neue, Clarendon

National Geographic Society

John M. Fahey, Jr., *President and Chief Executive
Officer;* Gilbert M. Grosvenor, *Chairman of the Board;*
Nina D. Hoffman, *Executive Vice President, President of
Book Publishing Group*

Staff for This Book

Nancy Laties Feresten, *Vice President, Editor-in-Chief
of Children's Books*
Virginia Ann Koeth, *Project Editor*
Bea Jackson, *Director of Design and Illustration*
David M. Seager, *Art Director*
Lori Epstein, National Geographic Image Sales,
Illustrations Editors
Jean Cantu, *Illustrations Specialist*
Priyanka Lamichhane, *Assistant Editor*
R. Gary Colbert, *Production Director*

Lewis R. Bassford, *Production Manager*
Maryclare Tracy, Nicole Elliott, *Manufacturing
Managers*
Maps, *Mapping Specialists, Ltd.*

For the Brown Reference Group, plc
Tim Cooke, *Editor*
Alan Gooch, *Book Designer*
Encompass Graphics, *Cartographers*

Photo Credits
Front cover © The Newark Museum/Art Resource, NY
Spine: © John S. Sfondilias/Shutterstock
Back cover: Figure: © Werner Forman/Art Resource,
NY; Background: © gds/zefa/Corbis

NGIC = National Geographic Image Collection.
1, © Maxwell Museum of Anthropology Alburquerque/
Werner Forman; 2–3, © Ira Block/NGIC; 4, © Ira
Block/NGIC; 5, © gds/zefa/Corbis; 6, © John S
Sfondillas/Shutterstock; 7, © gds/zefa/Corbis, © Ira
Blcok/NGIC; 10, © Arizona State Museum/Werner
Forman; 11t, © Werner Forman; 11b, © Maxwell
Museum of Anthropology Alburquerque/Werner
Forman; 12–13, © Ira Block/NGIC; 14t, © Dewitt
Jones/Corbis; 14b, © Ira Block/NGIC; 15, © Ira
Block/NGIC; 16t, © Ira Block/NGIC; 16b, © Dewitt
Jones/Corbis; 17, © University of Tucson Museum,
Arizona/Werner Forman; 18, © Jim Sugar/Corbis; 19,
© Ira Block/NGIC; 20–21, © Arizona State Museum/
Werner Forman; 22t, © Visuals Unlimited/Corbis; 22b,
© David Muench/Corbis; 23, © David Muench/Corbis;
24t, © Arizona State Museum/Werner Forman; 24b, ©
Arizona State Museum/Werner Forman; 25, © Jan-
Butchofsky-Houser/Corbis; 26, © Jim Zuckerman/
Corbis; 27, © D.Thompson/Ancient Art and
Architecture Collection Ltd; 28, © George H. Huey/
Corbis; 29, © Volkmar K.Wentzel/NGIC; 30–31, © Ira
Block/NGIC; 32, © Ira Block/NGIC; 33, © Kihn W.
Langdon/NGIC; 34–35, © Kinuko Y. Craft/NGIC;
36, © Mesa Verde National Park; 37, © Ira Block/NGIC;
38, © George H. Huey/Corbis; 39t, © Roy Anderson/
NGIC; 39b, © David Muench/Corbis; 40t, © Dewitt
Jones/Corbis; 40b, © Dr Frank C. Hibben/NGIC;
41, © NASA; 42, © Ira Block/NGIC; 43, © Ira
Block/NGIC; 44–45, © Werner Forman; 46, © Maxwell
Museum of Anthropology Alburquerque/Werner
Forman; 47, © Mesa Verde National Park; 48t, © Buddy
Mays/Corbis; 48b, © Tom Silver/Corbis; 49, © David
Muench/Corbis; 50, © Richard A. Cooke/Corbis; 51,
© George H. Huey/Corbis; 52, © Stephen Lekson; 53,
© Ken Abbott/University of Colorado, Boulder; 54–55,
© Ira Block/NGIC; 56, © George H. Huey/Corbis; 57,
© Joseph Sohm/Visions of America; 58, © Ira Block/
NGIC; 63, © Marilyn Angel Wynn/Nativestock Pictures/
Corbis.

Front cover: A pottery figure made by the Anasazi.
Page 1 and back cover: This black-and-white pitcher,
made around 1000, reflects the patterns of earlier
Anasazi basketwork.
Pages 2–3: Anasazi ruins on a high mesa in Arizona